WAKING to BREVITY

poems by

Sarah W. Bartlett

Finishing Line Press
Georgetown, Kentucky

WAKING to BREVITY

to my late husband Jim
who modeled a good life
and a good death
for us all

ACKNOWLEDGMENTS

I want to acknowledge my long-time friend and sister-poet, Anne Averyt,
whose dedication to poetry—including hers and mine—helped bring this
collection to fruition. For the many years these poems have been gestating,
and ultimately coming together, she provided endless encouragement,
editorial acumen, and creative cheerleading. Sadly, she did not live to hold
the physical book in her hands; yet her spirit infuses its final form, for which
I am eternally grateful.

Publisher: Leah Huete de Maines
Editor: Christen Kincaid
Cover Photo: Jim Hester
Author Photo: Peter Crawford
Cover Design: Sarah W. Bartlett

Order online: www.finishinglinepress.com
also available on amazon.com

Author inquiries and mail orders:
Finishing Line Press
PO Box 1626
Georgetown, Kentucky 40324
USA

A SarahJim2.0 creation

Contents

*... No more than a solemn waking
to brevity, to the lifting and falling away of attention, swiftly,
a time between times ... No more than that.*

—from "A Piece of the Storm" by Mark Strand
in *Blizzard of One: Poems*, Alfred A Knopf, NY, 1999

Prologue: Third Anniversary

Just as we dreamed it… sitting
here. Recalling hills climbed,
steep descents… The essence
of Us. Remembering.
More real than dreams
lost by your too-early death.

You made it just shy of 75
when the rest of us gathered at our
tiny cottage I now call home.
Did you sense laughter, tears flowing
memories, tender hugs, farewells?

You are here—your love of the sea,
boyish delight at bare feet in cool grass
or showering outdoors—our Cot
holding you deep in its bones.

It may not emit your laughter
or mirror your smile. But they are
here inside these walls
and my heart.
Not just when I need you,
but all ways. These, too,
I remember.

open

as a cave at night,
imagination sings
of desire arriving on wings
of stars, angels bearing
the single miracle
that can outlast time

The Rose

you start small
      curled
            unknowing yet

hopeful,
      with each unfurling
            more confident

slowly
      learning the shape
            of who you become

adversity
      need
            desire

feeding you
      feeding you
            feeding you

and still the rose
      unfurls
            all it has held

holding yet
      opening
            to what comes

I Married You

I married you
for all the wrong reasons,
charmed into collusion
with your savvy siblings;

by your naïveté,
hidden mines in your heart;
your desire and white socks
simple as the spilled sand
you thought I'd not see.

I was charmed too
by your assumptions of me:
conformity, my sweet surrender
to the kitchen
and you.

How wrong we both were
about the other. And yet
how right for each other.

(mirrored on Linda Pastan's poem of the same name, from *Queen
of a Rainy Country.* © W. W. Norton & Company, 2008)

Vision of Love

You wanted it all romantic nights,
candlelit strokes across the cheek
to carry you through your days.

But betrayal, loss score
the soft belly of desire, barbed
understories amass. We need

to accept what's become, find
tender regard to avoid—
and I mean this—silent despair.

Or we'll find both the beauty
and the pain—our love—dispersed.

Dig deep within our tangled truths.
Recall promises crafted once
in *faith ... hope ... love ...*

weaving more than half our lives.
Possibility hovers yet among burrs
in late afternoon's lingering

light, begs us to live as if we loved,
that indeed we might
at our last.

how our lives

move making
separate paths
yet twine together
formed while forming,
transparent, layered,
growing

Natural Rhythms

We bumble along with hope, good will,
instinct urging *onward* ...
       onward ...

We've learned to talk things through
on long morning walks, winter sun still
asleep; or in summer's sluggish heat.
With a half-glass of Malbec at dusk.
During restive hours from midnight
to dawn—when even owls have quieted,
the house dark—resuming hushed tones
under covers like sleep-over teens.

We've known the yearning tug of trust—
the wrench of withheld and dismissed,
deceit, the challenge to forgive—
and the toil of long years
for faith and hope to walk us
hand in hand to the end.

We argue, voices rising and falling
on the waves of our tolerance,
ability to open, desire to deepen.
We murmur, laugh, request, suggest—
along with pecks, hugs, and deep
soulful exchange—the language
that floats us on our years together,
sharing dreams of loving
and dying well.

Our evolving lives an elegant
amalgam of resolve
       of love.

A Lifetime Together, in Three Short Decades

Solstice night and a real estate deal. Mending
hearts. Words for a wedding. Snippets of hair—
red, blond, near-black—and a trio of milk teeth. Instinct
vs history. Parsing love languages. Late-life mother
with mid-career dad. Steep learning curves ahead.

Draft papers, contracts. Moving west, then back east.
Puerto Rico. Family. Mountain cabin summers.
Cot-by-the-sea blooming. Surgeries, trust, healing.
Wilderness camping, day hikes, adventures.
Photography. Poems. Time to grow, delve deep.

Healthcare reform. Travel notes, poems
photos and emails from abroad. Dream trips.
Retirement. Health records. End-of-life plans.
Gratitude letters, honors; farewells and hospice bills.
Love notes. Promises. Forgiveness. Peace.

Dusk

In the musty cool evening, moon rises
over the distant horizon ever nearer to home,

autumn's crisp crunch and scent encasing
memories in each crumbling leaf.

Love—what matters and what lasts year to year—
cycles from then to now and onward, reaching

both forward and back as the moon arcs,
circles, returns. May we, too, linger

in our rounds of light and dark, unknowing
enough to remain completely present.

there are signs

of impending tsunami.
Changing focus, outlook.
Ground shifting, unsettled.
Wind knocking one
sideways
from nowhere

Underground

You cannot always tell by looking what is happening,
the silent pain of loss coursing through you

loss of what has always been, never having
anticipated this sea-change of your body

your body once proudly worn through challenges
both mental and physical

the physical now beyond challenging,
newly morphed into impossibility

'impossible' being not what you believe
but mere hypothesis neither true nor tested;

yet you are tested now daily to discover
what still works—or not—over again

and again *who am I now?* forcing the need
to find 'normal' even though you look yourself

because you cannot always tell by looking
what is happening...

(inspired by Marge Piercy's poem, "The Seven of Pentacles," from *Circles on the Water,* Knopf, 1982)

Valentines Day

Learning you
have Parkinson's.
A downward slide
without cure.
At best,
slowed progress.

Mortality to mourn,
prepare for, resist.
How long do we have?
Twenty years?
or five?

At what point
will it become
too much?
A different Valentine,

this. Wrapped
as presence
to live

with grace
and dignity

what remains.

Tumble of Matins
Florence, Italy, 2012

Sunday morning's tumble of matins
invites us to explore Florence,
Tuscany's vineyards, Umbria's
olives. Our first test of optimism
and your limits
since PD's reveal.

Despite fatigue-shortened days,
all senses urge us
toward filling and tasting,
anticipations gratified
and grateful for each.

Yet photos fast-forward your age—
and dismay—beyond a decade,
PD's progress eclipsing our days,
boundaries, plans   our hope
for reprieve.

who could have known

our countless journeys—
of climb, scramble, fall, regroup—
across bald rock and stream
in ice, mud and sun ... or
how with grace we'd accept
what shifts beneath us

Beginning the End

How could either of us forget
June of '18, everything
taking us by surprise?
Assaults mounting
daily. Falls. Fractures.
Movement vs. healing.
Juggling dosages.
Dueling meds.
A quick descent
from independence
to off-the-cliff decline.

You rarely complain.
But your eyes.
Slumped shoulders. Lost
confidence, strength.
Your body's betrayal
just ahead of your mind's.
Life at the mercy
of randomness.
You choosing—
from narrowing options
you did not—to control
the rest of your life
till you can't.

Priority of Cake

For weeks now, you have been in pain
from so many falls, sacrum and spine
bearing the brunt. Though medically stable,

the pain migrates and little mitigates it
but distraction. So you sit, rock,
shift chair to bed, shuffle uphill

and back with the cane 'til now a mere prop
in the Bentwood stand. You slip in and out
of speech, read, catch strains of music,

news, outdoor adventure or weather drifting
across our grandson's laughter, romping dogs,
quick consults with our daughter about meals.

I check Paul's glucose level as the timer dings
for the cake we are baking
to welcome him to his new home.

Everything needs attention at once as you
who just asked for help wave your hand,
command *check the cake first!*

April Shower

After we navigate
the narrow yet
perilous chasm
between wall
and toilet,
launch your lanky
length over
tub walls
across the bench
awaiting you,

and after the necessary
ablutions, languid
yet thorough,
your eyes close

a tranquil ease
drifting through you
as you idle
on the bench

face lifted
to streaming warmth
infusing you with
desire
to linger
a bit longer.

no telling

had I known
that would be
the last time
we'd touch,
what more
I might have done

Last Rhumba

On the day you stopped eating, she
arrived. To say goodbye, yes. But also
to share the song she would have liked

for your dance at her wedding—
no date, place or partner in mind—but the wish
to have had that final rite of passage

with her dad. You crawled from your bed
grabbing hold of the moment, her hand.
Her song was one you and I had danced

under star-studded Westport nights on the deck,
recalling ballrooms from VT to PR, a dusty
college stage for *rueda salsa,* local studios

sliding with Argentine tango. Weddings,
bar mitzvahs, reunions—even hotel lobbies
where Latin beat or swing drew out our dancing feet,

our swaying bodies always drawing asides
those two are so in love, year after year after year.
Barefoot or high-heeled, whatever I wore, you

chose your soft black Italian leather shoes.
As now. You rummaged in the closet to find them,
dust them off and slip them shakily onto your feet

then shuffled across the carpet to lean
into the strong arms of our youngest. Cheek
to cheek you lurched side to side, steps slowly

returned to memory, creating one for her
as she held tight to her father,
her dream manifest.

I Do

I sit with you through weeks of discomfort
you toilet-seat-rooted 'til numb
together seeking any possible
lightness to the hard truth before us.

I watch your trembling fingers
tug the table edge toward you
rock fore/aft   fore/aft
up into my waiting arms.

I see your strained face set
to climb on the bed, seek
how to turn and where
put your arms.

I hear you beg me
to loose the razor wire
you feel slice your torso
in sleep.

I shield your unsteady shuffle
from hitting walls as you slide
silent, passed out.

I feel will drain from you, despair
and disquiet slip into slots
of lost laughter.

I trace the translucence
barely sheathing your body that quit,
now pleading release.

I read your closed eyes, all you have left
laser-focused on leaving.

I know what you want.
I remember my word.

I do.

Remember These Words

you mouth, barely
audible through lips
that hardly move

yet the intensity
of your intent
is clear, hand
clutching mine, eyes
pleading against time
running out. Calm
but insistent, you
want to teach
everyone you meet

even now, late
as it is.
Your final words
of advice, promise
and gentle urging
hang in silence
while I strain
to grasp them.
Although I don't
really know all
you said, I'll
remember your words
meant for me
at the end.
Your words meant,
finally, for me.

setting sun

each shifting kaleidoscope
richer, more expansive
than before. Then darkness.
Eyes still imaging crimson
ribboned sky blind to human urge
to preserve the ephemeral

Shrinking World

The day came when you said, *my world has become very small—*
our bedroom, bathroom, the toilet. But that was spacious
compared with the day, not so long after that
you struggled one last time onto the bed.
This is where I'm going to spend
the rest of my life, isn't it?
Less question than fact.
And it was. The rest
of your life but
three more
days.

After

Where am I
among the gaps
between then and now?

How can I even begin
to traverse a void
so vast?

For now all I can do
is sit here
with your memory

waiting
to find a new way
home.

Unexpected

Cooler than expected, the air
gives in to sun. Distant
traffic muffles in breeze rising
above the silence of dogs.

A lone seagull pierces inland twitter.
A neighbor speaks, red car passes by.
Ordinary moments of a weekend
in a quiet city enclave.

But I feel what is missing, the lurch
of your uneven gait beside me.

Smile instead at you striding up Sunset Ridge
as I scramble to reach you, perch side by side
to share water, G.O.R.P., laughter
as Loki drink-swims the icy stream...

Looking around, I see your absence
and my not-yet-coming-to-terms
that our plans are no more; yet
I go on. I return from my walk

deadhead the *Nova Zemla* by the door,
snip a newly-bloomed peony for the house,

enter the silence I have just left to find it
alive with sun, the comfort of the familiar
and your gentle presence still
warm in my heart.

like endless rain

that has swelled
lake, stream and field,
this continuous filling
emptied
will flow untold loss
in its wake

Flight Path

In the fading light
of a too-warm day
I cast about for a glimpse of you
at this intersection of so many
trips from home, you

determined to keep moving
toward the horizon of possibility
as you journeyed ahead.
I will the possibility
that your spirit hovers here

as I travel behind you
seeking murmurs of comfort
and courage to soften
the harsh reality of loss,
of opportunity missed.

If I whisper to you now,
will your spirit linger still
in the vapor of my breath, of
intention not yet lived, of desire
unfulfilled?

Inner Light

Always your curiosity
a light of *YES!*
to an openhearted life
refusing the dark.

The night you ceased food,
our candle-lit vigil
held you in light
reflecting your own.

Was it you, then,
this harvest moon?
A hovering presence
—shining, unknown—

yet palpably familiar
waking me
into its fleeting
embrace.

By day, the sun's shimmer
along the gray river.
A glimmer
of hope.

Your Hands

Your hands, generous
and firm, covered
my back. From our first

lingering hug
through nightly caress

that soothed me to rest
much as you
first moved me to love.

Your hands declared
first signs of PD

clenched tight
to your side, powerless
to unfurl.

Your hands waxed
and waned across years

lost and betrayed
by body and mind twisting
what you thought you knew.

Like the night I asked
for a rub; and you, startled

exclaimed "But I am."
Your hands weightless
whispers

missing the touch
I long for.

ABOUT PARKINSON'S DISEASE

Parkinson's Disease (PD) may manifest first as either frozen or random movement, and may not be apparent to the person to whom it is happening. Progressing at its own pace, PD moves unpredictably but inexorably toward decline of external, internal and eventually mental capacities. It can be mitigated by a series of medications depending on prominent symptoms, but has no cure. It may co-exist with its victim for brief or extended periods of time. Much as we try not to define ourselves by dis-ease, with PD it is virtually impossible not to. Because it's about witnessing steady decline and all that it takes with it.

At best, medications can slow PD's progress. Often, sadly, at the cost of increasing the impact of other conditions or causing interaction effects that can make even simple tasks of daily living unbearable. Only recently have potential causes of PD begun to be understood. But in living with it, one learns how to solve other problems. For us, it deepened our compassion and caring for one another. It taught us the life-sustaining power of humor. We both learned how to live with grace and presence; and when the time came to let go, to let go.

After myriad attempts over the years, Jim declared this 2010 picture of me his favorite. Looking at it deeply today, I try to see what he saw. A woman at ease with herself and at home in the natural world. I, who always identified as nurturer, have all this time been truly nurtured by the place I live and spend my days.

Nurturer and nurtured. These are the roots of my writing, my life, my relationships. Experienced and shared through a poetic lens, they express my profound gratitude for each gift.

Walking to Brevity is a heart-centered memoir of our last decade together when Jim and I were joined by an uninvited third party— Parkinson's Disease. One theme of these poems arises from our mutual commitment to improving patient care. Jim's curious mind kept me taking notes right up to the end. As his sensory mirror, I was able to add my own observations. Together, we sought to share what worked and what could be improved at both the systems and individual levels.

Also through these poems, I follow the early challenges and adventures of our later-in-life marriage as they morphed into a deepened mutual compassion. Just in time, as it happened, for our final decade together to pass in shared humor, problem-solving, and acceptance.

This is our journey, Jim's and mine. May it speak to your heart.